Ongwe oweh oadeh sigwa····deh
weso sigwa neh ga·ya·dos·hah dio·

FULTON PUBLIC LIBRARY
FULTON · NEW YORK

MY FIRST SPORTS

Volleyball

by Ray McClellan

BLASTOFF! READERS

4

BELLWETHER MEDIA • MINNEAPOLIS, MN

Note to Librarians, Teachers, and Parents:

Blastoff! Readers are carefully developed by literacy experts and combine standards-based content with developmentally appropriate text.

Level 1 provides the most support through repetition of high-frequency words, light text, predictable sentence patterns, and strong visual support.

Level 2 offers early readers a bit more challenge through varied simple sentences, increased text load, and less repetition of high-frequency words.

Level 3 advances early-fluent readers toward fluency through increased text and concept load, less reliance on visuals, longer sentences, and more literary language.

Level 4 builds reading stamina by providing more text per page, increased use of punctuation, greater variation in sentence patterns, and increasingly challenging vocabulary.

Level 5 encourages children to move from "learning to read" to "reading to learn" by providing even more text, varied writing styles, and less familiar topics.

Whichever book is right for your reader, Blastoff! Readers are the perfect books to build confidence and encourage a love of reading that will last a lifetime!

This edition first published in 2011 by Bellwether Media, Inc.

No part of this publication may be reproduced in whole or in part without written permission of the publisher. For information regarding permission, write to Bellwether Media, Inc., Attention: Permissions Department, 5357 Penn Avenue South, Minneapolis, MN 55419.

Library of Congress Cataloging-in-Publication Data
McClellan, Ray.
Volleyball / by Ray McClellan.
    p. cm. – (Blastoff! readers: My first sports)
Includes bibliographical references and index.
Summary: "Simple text and full-color photography introduce beginning readers to the sport of volleyball. Developed by literacy experts for students in grades two through five"–Provided by publisher.
ISBN 978-1-60014-464-6 (hardcover : alk. paper)
  1. Volleyball–Juvenile literature. I. Title.
GV1015.34.M33 2010
796.325–dc22   2010000783

Text copyright © 2011 by Bellwether Media, Inc. BLASTOFF! READERS and associated logos are trademarks and/or registered trademarks of Bellwether Media, Inc. ·

Printed in the United States of America, North Mankato, MN.
080110   1162

Contents

What Is Volleyball?

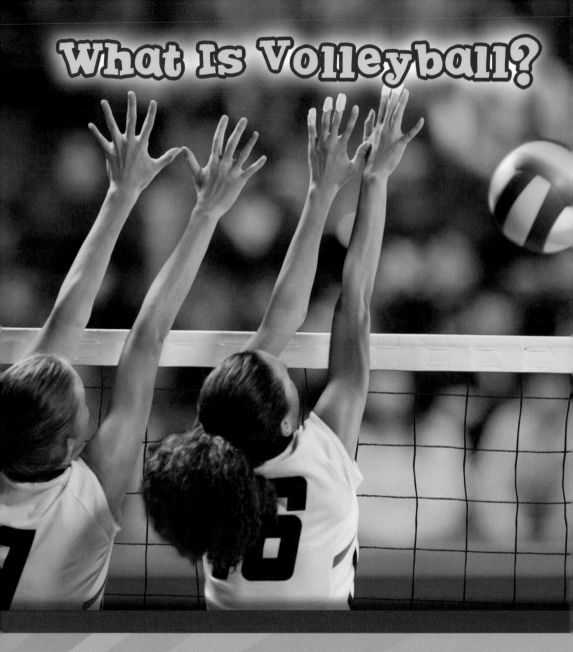

Volleyball is a team sport in which teams hit a ball back and forth over a net. William G. Morgan invented the sport in Massachusetts in 1895. He called it **mintonette**.

People liked how teams had to **volley** the ball. They started calling the sport volleyball.

In time, volleyball spread around the world. The first World Championship was held in 1949. In 1964, volleyball became a sport in the **Olympics**.

In the 1990s and 2000s, the popularity of **beach volleyball** created more interest in the sport.

Each volleyball team has six players.
The teams stand on opposite sides of a net.
They hit a ball back and forth over the net.

Each point begins with a **serve**. The serving team scores a point by getting the ball to touch the ground on the other team's side of the court. They also score if the other team hits the ball out-of-bounds.

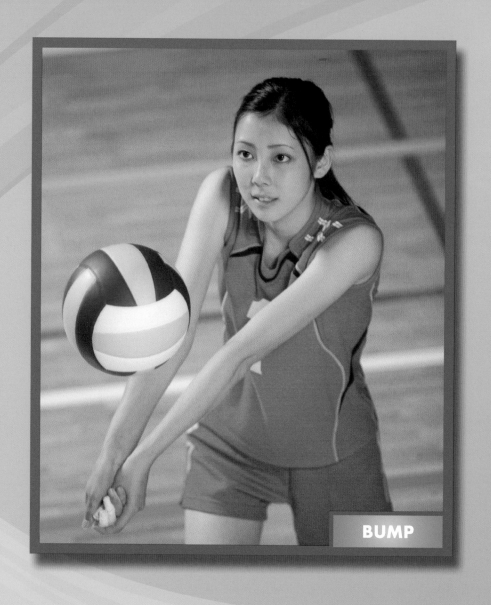

BUMP

The receiving team has three hits to **bump**, **set**, or **spike** the ball back over the net. A bump is a hit made to pop the ball into the air.

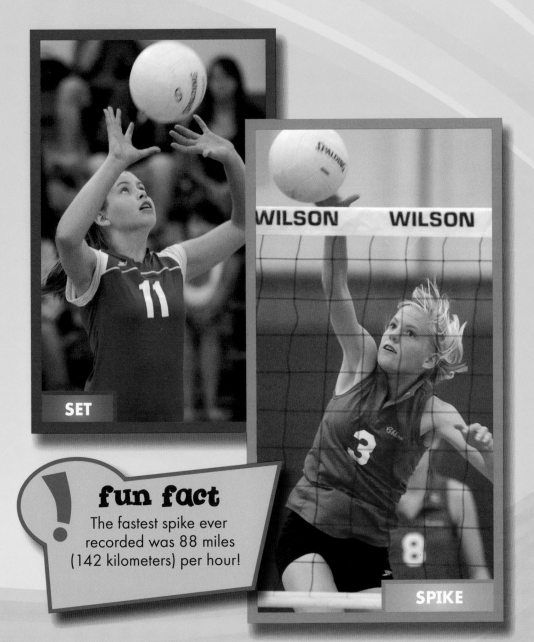

SET

WILSON WILSON

SPIKE

fun fact

The fastest spike ever
recorded was 88 miles
(142 kilometers) per hour!

Sets are used to place the ball above and
near the net. A spike is a hard downward
hit over the net.

fun fact

Since a team has to win by 2 points, some games took a long time. Most leagues now cap scoring around 35 or 40.

A **side-out** is when a team gets the serve. The team's players rotate positions. In **rally scoring**, either team can score a point after a serve.

Most official games go to 25 points.
Teams must win by at least 2 points.

Volleyball Equipment

Teams need some basic equipment to play volleyball. The ball they use is made of either real or **synthetic** leather.

Adult volleyballs measure about 26 inches (66 centimeters) around and weigh about 9.5 ounces (270 grams). Youth volleyballs are slightly smaller and lighter.

fun fact
Players often dive to reach a ball. They wear knee pads so they do not hurt their knees on the hard floor.

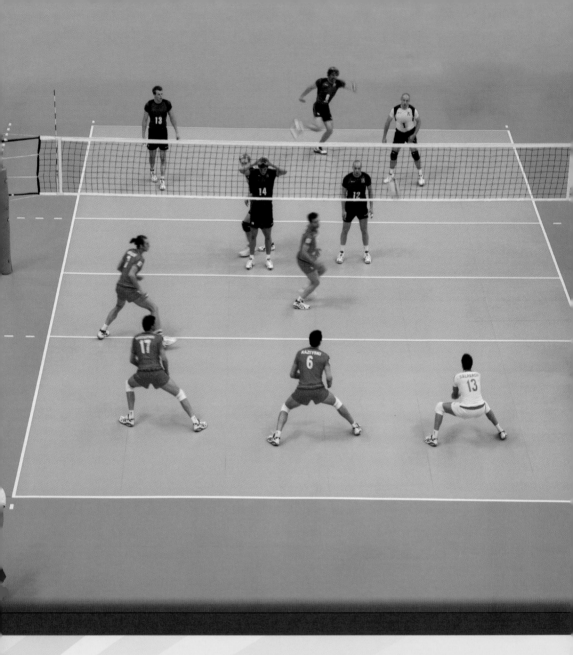

Teams also need a court with a net.
A standard volleyball court is 59 feet (18
meters) long and 29.5 feet (9 meters) wide.

A standard net stands almost 8 feet (2.4 meters) tall for men. For women, it is just over 7 feet 4 inches (2.2 meters).

Volleyball Today

Around the world, people of all ages play volleyball. Some enjoy community leagues.

Others play in high school, college, or even in European professional leagues.

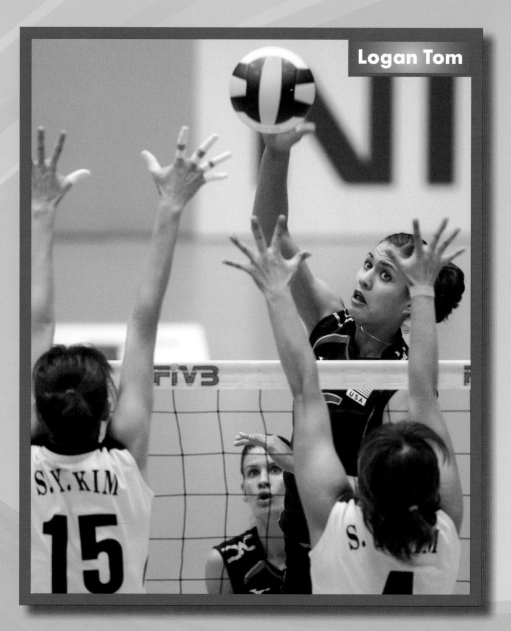

Logan Tom

The highest level of volleyball is played at the Olympics. Stars like Logan Tom, Nancy Metcalf, and Lloy Ball inspire fans to work on their own bumps, sets, and spikes.

Lloy Ball

! fun fact

The United States men's volleyball team won the gold medal at the 2008 Olympics. Brazil won the gold in women's volleyball.

Volleyball is a game almost anyone can enjoy. Are you ready for the challenge?

Glossary

beach volleyball—a version of volleyball in which teams of two compete on a sand court

bump—a hit designed to get the ball up in the air; a bump is sometimes called a pass.

mintonette—the original name given to the game of volleyball

Olympics—an event in which athletes from countries around the world gather to compete in sporting events

rally scoring—the method of scoring in which either team can score a point; before 1999, only the serving team could score.

serve—to begin a point by hitting the ball from the back of the court over the net

set—a hit that puts the ball close to the net for a spike

side-out—to gain the serve by winning a point

spike—a hard downward hit from close to the net

synthetic—artificial, or made by people

volley—to hit a ball back and forth over a net

To Learn More

AT THE LIBRARY
Crossingham, John. *Spike it Volleyball*. New York, N.Y.: Crabtree Publishing, 2008.

Evdokimoff, Natasha. *Volleyball*. New York, N.Y.: Weigl Publishers, 2000.

Kelly, Zachary A. *Volleyball: Fitness and Training*. Vero Beach, Fla.: Rourke Publishing, 1998.

ON THE WEB
Learning more about volleyball is as easy as 1, 2, 3.

1. Go to www.factsurfer.com.

2. Enter "volleyball" into the search box.

3. Click the "Surf" button and you will see a list of related Web sites.

With factsurfer.com, finding more information is just a click away.

Index

The images in this book are reproduced through the courtesy of: David Davis, front cover; Jun Tsukuda/ Photolibrary, pp. 4-5, 13, 14, 19; Sports Illustrated/Getty Images, pp. 6, 17, 21; AFP/Getty Images, pp. 7, 8-9, 20; Aflo Sport/Masterfile, p. 10; Jim Cayer/Cayer's Sports Action Photography, p. 11 (left, right); Antonio Ros, p. 12; Juan Martinez, pp. 15, 18; Losevsky Pavel, p. 16.